Spotlight on
Australia

Bobbie Kalman

Crabtree Publishing Company

www.crabtreebooks.com

Spotlight On My Country

Created by Bobbie Kalman

For our friend Priscilla Baker, and in memory of Karl Baker,
with love from Peter and Bobbie.
We hope this book brings back wonderful memories.

**Author and
Editor-in-Chief**
Bobbie Kalman

Editor
Robin Johnson

Photo research
Bobbie Kalman
Crystal Sikkens

Design
Katherine Kantor
Samantha Crabtree (cover)

Production coordinator
Katherine Kantor

Illustrations
Barbara Bedell: page 15
Katherine Kantor: pages 4, 5, 6, 8, 10, 18, 24
Robert MacGregor: page 12

Photographs
© BigStockPhoto.com: pages 7 (top), 19 (top right),
 25 (middle)
© Dreamstime.com: pages 19 (bottom left except inset),
 28 (top left)
© iStockphoto.com: pages 7 (bottom), 16 (bottom right),
 17 (except bottom left), 27 (bottom left), 29 (top right)
© 2008 Jupiterimages Corporation: pages 16 (middle right),
 20 (top), 21, 25 (top right), 31 (bottom right)
© Shutterstock.com: back cover, pages 1, 3, 5, 8, 9, 10, 11, 12, 13,
 14, 15, 16 (top left and bottom left), 17 (bottom left),
 18 (background), 19 (background, bottom left inset, and
 bottom right), 20 (bottom), 22, 23, 24, 25 (top left and bottom),
 26, 27 (except bottom left), 28 (bottom left and right),
 29 (except top right), 30, 31 (top and bottom left)
Other images by Digital Stock and Digital Vision

Library and Archives Canada Cataloguing in Publication

Kalman, Bobbie, 1947-
    Spotlight on Australia / Bobbie Kalman.

(Spotlight on my country)
Includes index.
ISBN 978-0-7787-3453-6 (bound).--ISBN 978-0-7787-3479-6 (pbk.)

    1. Australia--Juvenile literature. I. Title. II. Series.

DU96.K25 2008   j994   C2008-901219-4

Library of Congress Cataloging-in-Publication Data

Kalman, Bobbie.
  Spotlight on Australia / Bobbie Kalman.
    p. cm. -- (Spotlight on my country)
  Includes index.
  ISBN-13: 978-0-7787-3479-6 (pbk. : alk. paper)
  ISBN-10: 0-7787-3479-X (pbk. : alk. paper)
  ISBN-13: 978-0-7787-3453-6 (reinforced library binding : alk. paper)
  ISBN-10: 0-7787-3453-6 (reinforced library binding : alk. paper)
  1. Australia--Juvenile literature. I. Title.
DU96.K36 2008
994--dc22
                                        2008006378

Crabtree Publishing Company
www.crabtreebooks.com   1-800-387-7650

**Published in Canada
Crabtree Publishing**
616 Welland Ave.
St. Catharines, Ontario
L2M 5V6

**Published in the United States
Crabtree Publishing**
PMB16A
350 Fifth Ave., Suite 3308
New York, NY 10118

**Published in the United Kingdom
Crabtree Publishing**
White Cross Mills
High Town, Lancaster
LA1 4XS

**Published in Australia
Crabtree Publishing**
386 Mt. Alexander Rd.
Ascot Vale (Melbourne)
VIC 3032

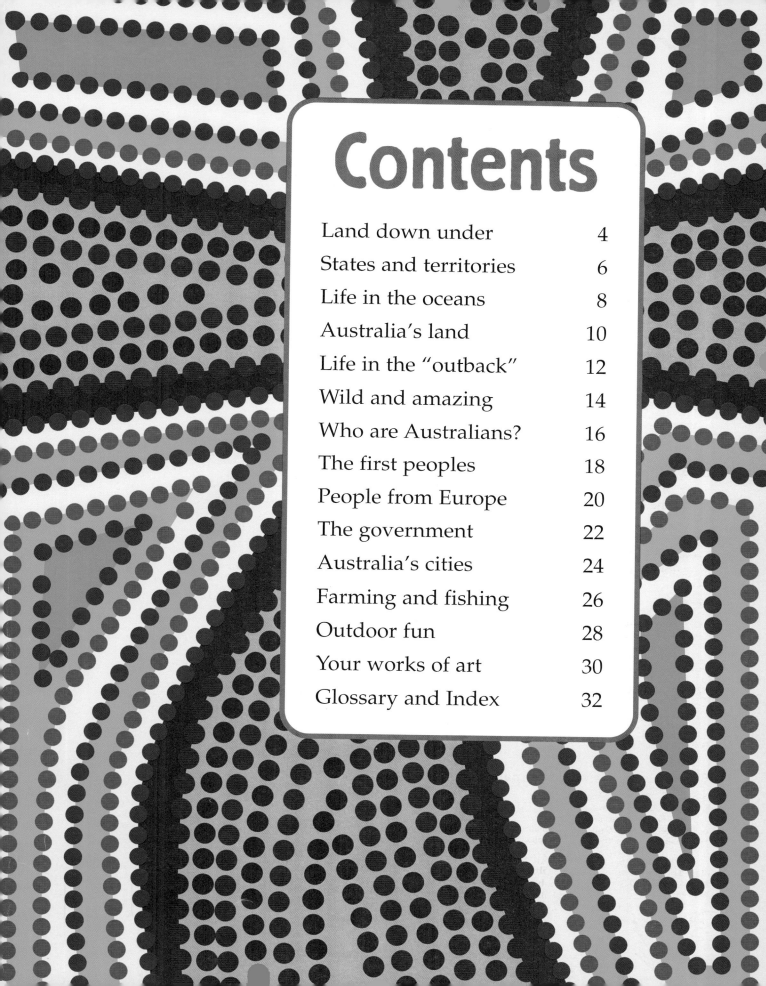

Contents

Land down under	4
States and territories	6
Life in the oceans	8
Australia's land	10
Life in the "outback"	12
Wild and amazing	14
Who are Australians?	16
The first peoples	18
People from Europe	20
The government	22
Australia's cities	24
Farming and fishing	26
Outdoor fun	28
Your works of art	30
Glossary and Index	32

Land down under

Australia is a **country**. A country is an area of land with people. A country has **laws**, or rules, that its people must follow. A country also has **borders** that separate it from other countries. Australia does not need borders. It has **oceans** all around it. Oceans are huge areas of salty water. There are also many **seas** around Australia. A sea is a small part of an ocean that has land around it.

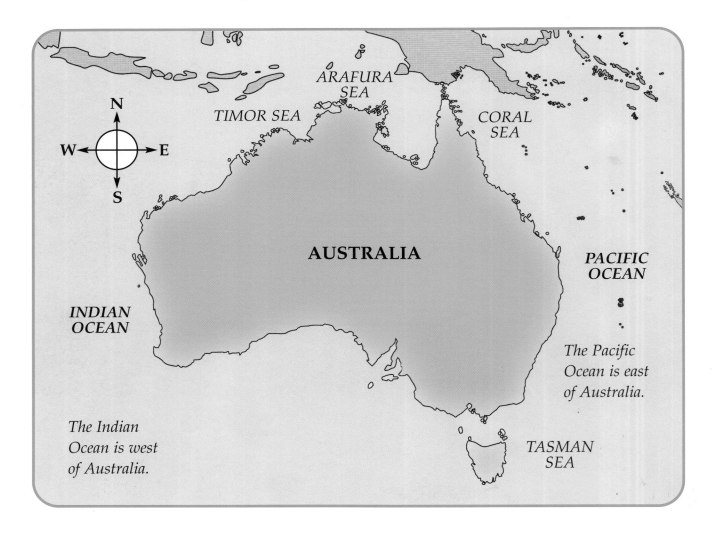

N
W E
S

TIMOR SEA

ARAFURA SEA

CORAL SEA

AUSTRALIA

INDIAN OCEAN

PACIFIC OCEAN

The Pacific Ocean is east of Australia.

The Indian Ocean is west of Australia.

TASMAN SEA

At the bottom of Earth

Australia is part of the **continent** of Australia and Oceania. A continent is a huge area of land. Australia is called the "land down under." It is below the **equator**. The equator is an imaginary circle around the middle of Earth. The equator divides Earth into two parts. Australia is in the bottom part of Earth, called the **Southern Hemisphere**.

This girl is pointing to Australia. Australia is at the bottom of the globe.

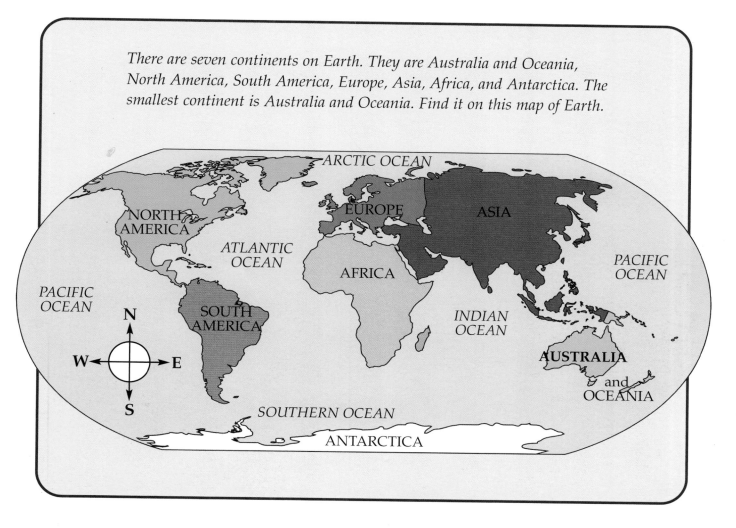

There are seven continents on Earth. They are Australia and Oceania, North America, South America, Europe, Asia, Africa, and Antarctica. The smallest continent is Australia and Oceania. Find it on this map of Earth.

ARCTIC OCEAN

NORTH AMERICA

EUROPE

ASIA

ATLANTIC OCEAN

AFRICA

PACIFIC OCEAN

PACIFIC OCEAN

SOUTH AMERICA

INDIAN OCEAN

N
W E
S

AUSTRALIA and OCEANIA

SOUTHERN OCEAN

ANTARCTICA

States and territories

Australia is made up of a **mainland** and many **islands**. The mainland is the large land area of Australia. Australia has six **states**, two mainland **territories**, and some smaller territories. A state is an area of a country that has its own **government**. A government makes laws and important decisions for its people. A territory is an area that is run by a country's **federal**, or main, government. Australian Capital Territory and Northern Territory are like states. They have their own governments.

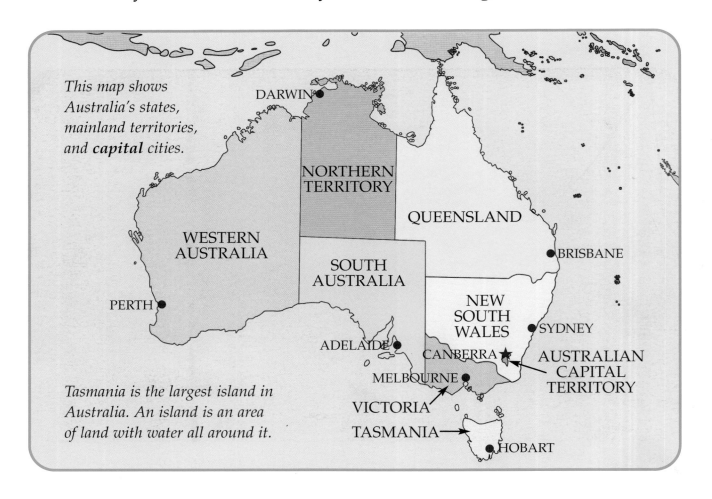

*This map shows Australia's states, mainland territories, and **capital** cities.*

DARWIN

NORTHERN TERRITORY

QUEENSLAND

WESTERN AUSTRALIA

SOUTH AUSTRALIA

•BRISBANE

NEW SOUTH WALES

PERTH•

ADELAIDE•

CANBERRA

•SYDNEY

AUSTRALIAN CAPITAL TERRITORY

MELBOURNE

Tasmania is the largest island in Australia. An island is an area of land with water all around it.

VICTORIA

TASMANIA→

•HOBART

A long coast

Australia's mainland has **coasts** all around it. A coast is an area where land meets an ocean. Australia's coasts have long sandy beaches, rocky shores, and **cliffs**. Cliffs are tall, steep rocks. Australia's big cities are found along its coasts. The city in the picture below is Sydney.

*The Twelve Apostles are **pillars**, or tall rocks. They were once part of the cliffs on the coast of Victoria. The pillars were cut away from the cliffs by ocean waves and wind.*

*Sydney is a big city on Australia's east coast. Its **harbor** is crowded with many boats.*

Life in the oceans

The largest coral reef on Earth is the Great Barrier Reef. It is the area on this map that is shown in pink.

Many kinds of animals live in the oceans around Australia. Some live in **coral reefs**. Coral reefs are huge underwater structures found near coasts. They look like rocks with plants growing on them, but they are not rocks or plants. Coral reefs are made up of groups of tiny animals called **coral polyps**.

More than 350 kinds of sharks live in the Great Barrier Reef. Many other kinds of fish and sea creatures also live in the reef. The sharks eat the smaller fish.

8

Blue-spotted rays live in the Great Barrier Reef.

Dolphins swim and play in and above the reef.

Sea turtles live in the Great Barrier Reef.

clownfish

sea anemone

Clownfish and sea anemones live in the reef.

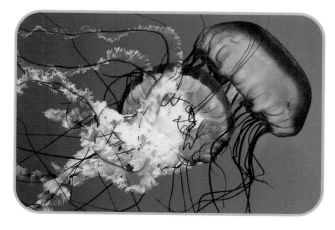

Sea jellies of all kinds live in the oceans around the reefs. These jellies are called sea nettles.

Many people **scuba dive** in the Great Barrier Reef. Does this diver know that he has company?

Australia's land

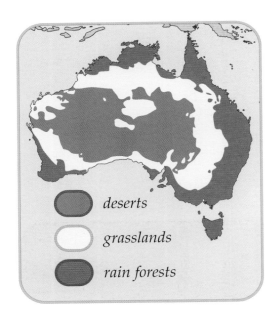

deserts

grasslands

rain forests

Australia has different **landscapes**. A landscape is how land looks. The middle part of Australia is made up of dry, hot areas called **deserts**. Around the deserts are **grasslands**. Grasslands have long grasses with bushes and some trees. Near the coasts of Australia, there are **rain forests**. There are mountains throughout Australia.

Tropical rain forests grow in the northern part of Australia. Tropical means hot and *humid*, or wet. In the north, the weather is always hot. It rains a lot for half of the year.

Cooler in the south

Most of Australia is warm all year long. Victoria, Tasmania, and parts of New South Wales are cooler than the rest of the country is, however. They even get some snow in winter.

The Cradle Mountains in Tasmania have snow on their tops in winter.

*The Greater Blue Mountains Area is in New South Wales. It has tall cliffs, deep **valleys**, caves, and **swamps**. It also has interesting **rock formations**. (See page 13.) The three rocks below are called the Three Sisters.*

Three Sisters

Life in the "outback"

The "**outback**" is an area of land that stretches across most of Australia. It is made up mainly of deserts. Very few people live in this hot, dry area of the country. Many kinds of animals live in the outback, however.

THE OUTBACK

•*Uluru*

Bearded dragons are lizards that live in the outback. They find plants and insects to eat there.

Red kangaroos live in the outback. They can go for long periods of time without water.

Sturt's desert pea is one of Australia's best-known wildflowers. It grows in the outback.

Uluru

Rock formations

Australia has many large rock formations. A rock formation is a rock with an unusual shape. The most famous rock in Australia is Uluru, shown above. It is one of the largest rocks on Earth. Uluru is found in the Simpson Desert in the outback.

Wild and amazing

Australia has thousands of kinds of plants that are not found anywhere else on Earth. There are trees, flowers, and other plants that are truly different and amazing. Australia's animals are also unusual. Some of the wild animals that live in Australia do not live in other countries.

Huge eucalyptus trees grow in Australia. Koalas climb these tall trees and eat the leaves that grow on them. Koalas eat a lot of leaves!

This flower is called a kangaroo paw. It grows only in parts of Western Australia.

Marsupials and monotremes

Australia has many animals called **marsupials**. Marsupials are **mammals**. Most marsupial mothers feed and carry their babies in pouches on their bodies. Kangaroos and koalas are marsupials with pouches. Other unusual animals are **monotremes**. Monotremes are mammals that lay eggs instead of giving birth. Echidnas and platypuses are monotremes.

An echidna mother lays an egg into a pouch on her body. After the egg hatches, the baby drinks its mother's milk inside the pouch.

A Tasmanian devil is a marsupial that lives in Tasmania. It is about the size of a small dog.

A quokka is a small marsupial. It is about the size of a cat. There are not many quokkas left on Earth.

*A duck-billed platypus is a monotreme that looks like a duck. It lays eggs inside a **burrow**, or hole.*

15

Who are Australians?

This boy is an Australian Aboriginal.

There are more than 20 million people in Australia. People who live in Australia are called Australians. The first Australians were **Aboriginals**, or native peoples. Today, most Australians have English, Irish, or Scottish **ancestors**. Most speak English.

This Australian is part Asian.

This child's ancestors are Irish.

These girls are Chinese Australians.

G'day mate!

"G'day mate!" is how Australians greet their friends. Australians are very friendly! They welcome people from all over the world to their country. People from Europe, Asia, Africa, North America, and South America have come to live in Australia.

This child's face is painted like an Australian flag. You do not have to wear a flag to be an Australian!

These people may not look the same, but they are all Australians!

The first peoples

Aboriginals first came to Australia from Asia about 60,000 years ago. More than 400 groups of Aboriginals lived in Australia. Some groups were **nomadic**. Nomadic peoples travel from place to place in search of food and water. Some Aboriginals who lived near the coasts were not nomadic. They found food in one place and lived there.

Torres Strait Islanders

Another group of people came to Australia about 12,000 years ago. These people came from New Guinea. They **settled** on the islands off the northeast coast of Australia. These Australians are known as the Torres Strait Islanders.

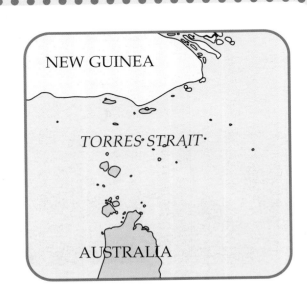

Practicing traditions

Today, most Aboriginals live in cities and towns. Some still live the way Aboriginals lived long ago, however. They travel from place to place and practice their **traditions**. Traditions are ways and beliefs that have been practiced for many years. Some of the traditions are passed down through ceremonies such as **corroborees**. Corroborees are for celebrating important events in life and for giving thanks.

The man above is talking about the Dreaming. The Dreaming consists of stories from long ago, in the time of the first ancestors. It tells how the land, animals, and people were created.

During corroborees, people paint their bodies with patterns that were used long ago.

Boomerangs were once used by Aboriginals for hunting. Today, they are used in sporting events.

People from Europe

These English prisoners are being loaded onto a ship that will take them to Australia.

People from Europe sailed to Australia in the 1600s, but they did not stay. Years later, an explorer named James Cook claimed Australia as an English **colony**. At that time, England had many prisoners and not enough jails. It began using Australia as a **penal colony**, or a great big jail. The first ship filled with prisoners and prison guards arrived in Australia in 1788. The prisoners were forced to build bridges and buildings and to plant **crops**. Crops are plants grown to be used by people.

Port Arthur is a prison in Tasmania. It was once used to hold England's most dangerous prisoners.

20

Free settlers

In the 1830s, people from England, Ireland, Scotland, and Germany came to live in Australia. They were not prisoners. They were free **settlers**. A settler is a person who lives in an area where there are not many people. Many of the settlers became **squatters**. Squatters take over land that they do not own. Many Aboriginals were killed trying to keep the squatters off native lands.

Thousands of free settlers sailed to Australia to start new lives. They traveled on big ships.

England sent explorers Robert Burke and William Wills to Australia to find new land for settlers. The explorers were not prepared for the heat of the outback. They died in the desert.

Caroline Chisholm helped women who came to Australia on their own. She found them places to live and trained them for jobs.

The government

Australia is a **commonwealth**. A commonwealth is a country that has its own government but is also connected with another country. The Queen of England is Australia's queen, but she does not rule Australia. Australia's government makes the decisions for its people. The **Prime Minister** is the head of the Australian government.

Union Flag

The blue color, the big star, and the Union Flag on Australia's flag all stand for Great Britain.

Happy Australia Day

January 26 is Australia Day. It is one of the biggest holidays of the year. On this day, Australians celebrate their country and its people.

Australia is a democracy

Australia is a **democracy**. In a democracy, people choose their government leaders by **voting** for them. Australia's leaders are **elected**, or chosen, by the people of Australia. Australia's federal government is a **parliament**. It is made up of two government **houses**, or groups. They are the Senate and the House of Representatives.

Australians vote for their leaders. To vote is to choose one person from a list of people.

Australia's federal government meets in the Parliament House in Canberra. Canberra is the capital of Australia.

The House of Representatives meets in this room of the Parliament House.

Australia's cities

Australia's most important cities are shown on this map. They are the capital cities.

Most Australians live in cities. Australia's big cities are found on the coasts, where the weather is mild. Sydney is the largest and oldest city in Australia. Some of the other cities in Australia are Melbourne, Perth, Brisbane, Adelaide, and Hobart. Canberra is a small **inland** city. Inland means it is not on a coast.

Brisbane is the third-largest city in Australia. The Brisbane River divides the city.

Melbourne is the second-largest city in Australia. It is called the Garden City. It has many parks.

Hobart is Tasmania's largest city. Behind Hobart is Mount Wellington.

(right) The most famous building in Australia is the Sydney Opera House. Its roof was built to look like the sails of a ship.

(below) Perth is on the west coast of Australia. It is far from any other city. Perth is **isolated**, or on its own.

25

Farming and fishing

Grapes grown in Australia are made into red and white wines. The wines are sold in countries all over the world.

Most of Australia's land is too hot and dry for farming. People still grow many kinds of crops, however. Farmers in Australia grow grains such as wheat, rye, and barley. Different fruits and vegetables, as well as sugar cane and peanuts, are also grown. On Australian **ranches**, or large farms, animals such as sheep and **cattle** are raised. Both the farm animals and the crops were brought to Australia from Europe long ago.

Rapeseed, or canola, grows in Australia. Canola oil comes from the seeds of these yellow flowers.

There are ten times as many sheep in Australia as there are people! Sheep are raised on huge ranches called **stations**. The sheep are raised for their meat and wool. Australia **produces**, or makes, more wool than any other country does. The wool is called Merino wool.

Cattle are also raised on stations. They are raised for their beef. Much of Australia's beef is sold to other countries.

Australians catch all kinds of fish in the oceans and seas. They also trap lobster and shrimp.

Hamburgers, french fries, and onion rings are favorite foods in Australia. Fish and chips are also very popular.

Australians often cook their seafood on barbecues. These shrimp are cooking on the "barbie."

Outdoor fun

*These students are on a school trip.
They are visiting a lighthouse.*

Australians spend a lot of time outdoors. The weather is usually warm, and most people live near coasts. There are many ways to have fun in Australia. Which of these Australian outdoor activities would you like to try?

*These children are going for a camel ride.
There are many camels in Australia's outback.*

wallaby

This young boy is hiking in a grassy area called "the bush." Will he see a wallaby there? A wallaby is a small marsupial.

Australians spend a lot of time at the beach. They even go on Christmas Day! In Australia, Christmas is in summer.

This girl is decorating a Christmas tree made of sticks on a quiet beach.

Many people surf in Australia's huge waves.

Tubing is also fun!

In surfboat rowing races, people race to a spot in the ocean and then back again. The waves are rough!

Your works of art

Aboriginal art is very colorful. It is also fun to make! Artists use a lot of dots and **geometric** shapes. You can make your own works of art. Use the pictures on these pages to get started.

Aboriginals painted pictures of animals on tree bark. They used dots, stripes, triangles, diamonds, circles, squares, ovals, and zigzags to create their art.

Find these shapes in the lizard, turtle, and kangaroo pictures on this page. Then use the shapes to make your own works of art. Have fun!

Use dots to make a simple design, such as the one above, or a picture of an animal, such as the turtle below. Use brightly colored dots to create your pictures.

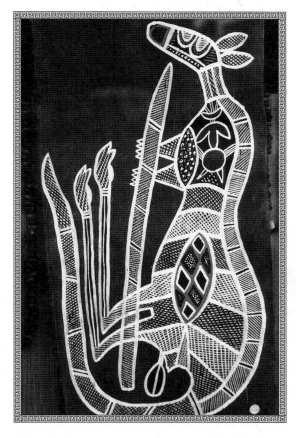

This kangaroo was painted on tree bark. It has many lines and shapes. You can make a picture like this, too. Hop to it!

31

Glossary

Note: Some boldfaced words are defined where they appear in the book.

Aboriginal A person who is first to live in an area

ancestor Someone who lived long ago and from whom another is descended

capital The city in which the government of a country, state, or territory is located

cattle Cows and oxen that people raise for their meat, milk, or hides

colony An area ruled by a country that is far away

commonwealth An area with its own government, but which is connected with another country, such as England

coral reef An area of the ocean that is made up of the coverings of live coral polyps and the skeletons of dead corals

desert A hot, dry area of land

geometric Made up of simple lines and shapes, such as circles and triangles

harbor An area of water near a coast where boats are protected from wind and waves

mammal An animal that is born, has hair or fur, and drinks its mother's milk

marsupial A mammal that grows in its mother's pouch after it is born and drinks its mother's milk there

monotreme A mammal that hatches from an egg and drinks mother's milk

outback A hot, dry desert area of Australia, where very few people live

parliament A government that is made up of elected and non-elected members

rain forest A forest that gets a lot of rain for part of the year or all of the year

scuba dive To swim under water while wearing a tank of air

settle To make a home and live in a place where few other people live

swamp An area of wet land that has trees, bushes, and other plants growing in it

valley A low area of land with mountains or hills around it

Index

Aboriginals 16, 18-19, 21, 30
animals 8, 12, 14-15, 19, 26, 30, 31
art 30-31
cities 6, 7, 19, 24-25
coasts 7, 8, 10, 18, 24, 25, 28
continents 5

crops 20, 26
deserts 10, 12, 13, 21
England 20, 21, 22
flags 17, 22
food 18, 27
government 6, 22-23
grasslands 10
Great Barrier Reef 8-9
islands 6, 18

maps 4, 5, 6, 8, 10, 12, 18, 24
mountains 10, 11
oceans 4, 5, 7, 8, 9, 27, 29
outback 12-13, 21, 28
people 4, 6, 9, 12, 16-19, 20, 21, 22, 23, 26, 27, 28, 29

plants 8, 12, 14, 20
rain forests 10
ranches 26, 27
rock formations 11, 13
states 6
Sydney 7, 24
Tasmania 6, 11, 15, 20, 24, 25
territories 6